Classifying Mammals

ANDREW SOLWAY

Heinemann Library
Chicago, Illinois

Originated by Dot Gradations
Printed in Hong Kong, China by Wing King Tong

07 06 05 04 03
10 9 8 7 6 5 4 3 2 1

Library of Congress Cataloging-in-Publication Data
Solway, Andrew.
    Classifying mammals / Andrew Solway.
        p. cm. -- (Classifying living things)
Summary: Explains what mammals are and how they differ from other animals, with an overview of the life cycle of a variety of mammals, including pouched mammals, sea mammals, flying mammals, and humans. Includes bibliographical references (p.) and index.
    ISBN 1-4034-0847-5 (lib. bdg.-hardcover) -- ISBN 1-4034-3347-X (pbk.)
    1. Mammals--Classification--Juvenile literature. 2. Mammals--Juvenile literature. [1. Mammals.] I. Title. II. Series.
    QL708 .S66 2003
    599--dc21

                                            2002015405

Acknowledgments
The publishers would like to thank the following for permission to reproduce photographs: p. 4 Corbis/Richard du Toit; pp. 5, 20 Digital Stock; p. 6 Nature Picture Library/Hanne and Jens Eriksen; p. 7 Natural History Museum; p. 9 Nature Picture Library/Staffan Widstrand; p. 10 Oxford Scientific Films/E.R.Degginner; p. 11 Bruce Coleman/John Cancalosi; p. 12 Corbis; p. 13 Corbis/Roger Tidman; p. 14 Oxford Scientific Films/Mary Plage; p. 15 Oxford Scientific Films; p. 16 Oxford Scientific Films/Tim Shepherd; p. 17 Oxford Scientific Films/Paul Franklin; p. 18 Nature Picture Library/Francois Savigny; p. 19 Nature Picture Library/Dan Burton; p. 21 Digital Vision; p. 22 Nature Picture Library/Pete Oxford; pp. 23, 25 Bruce Coleman/Jorg and Petra Wegner; p. 24 Nature Picture Library/Staffan Widstrand; p. 26 Bruce Coleman/Gunter Kohler; p. 27 RSPCA; p. 28 Harcourt Index; p. 29 Bruce Coleman/Alain Compost.

Cover photograph of zebras at a watering hole, reproduced with permission of Nature Picture Library.

For Harriet, Eliza and Nicholas.

The publishers would like to thank Catherine Armstrong, museum educator, for her assistance in the preparation of this book.

Every effort has been made to contact copyright holders of any material reproduced in this book. Any omissions will be rectified in subsequent printings if notice is given to the publishers.

Some words are shown in bold, **like this.** You can find out what they mean by looking in the glossary.

Contents

The Variety of Life

Think of an animal. What's the first one that comes to mind? Chances are, the animal you think of is a mammal. Pets such as cats and dogs, most of our farm animals, lions, zebras, elephants, mice, dolphins, and of course humans—all these and more are mammals. Wherever you look around the world, most of the large animals are mammals.

Scientists can identify thousands of different kinds, or **species,** of mammals, ranging from tiny pygmy shrews to huge blue whales. To try and understand how all these different animals are related to each other, scientists classify them, or sort them into groups.

Sorting the living world

When you sort things, they become easier to think about and understand. Scientists try to classify living things in a way that shows how closely one group of animals or plants is related to another. To do this, they compare groups of living things with each other. They look at everything about a living thing, from its color and shape to the **genes** inside its **cells.** They also look at **fossils,** which give them clues about how living things have changed over time. Then they use all this information to sort the millions of different living things into groups.

Mammals come in all shapes and sizes.

A species is a single kind of animal or plant, such as a dormouse or a buttercup. Species that are very similar to each other (for instance, different species of mice) are put together in a larger group called a **genus**. Genera that are similar to each other are grouped into **families,** and similar families make up larger groups called **orders**. Closely related orders are grouped into **classes,** classes are grouped into **phyla,** and finally, phyla are grouped into huge groups called kingdoms. Plants, for example, make up one kingdom, while animals make up another.

Scientific names

Many living things have a common name, which can be different in different languages. But when scientists classify living things, they give each species a two-part scientific name, which is the same all over the world. The first part of the scientific name is the genus that the creature belongs to, and the second part is its species. Leopards, for example, have the scientific name *Panthera pardus*.

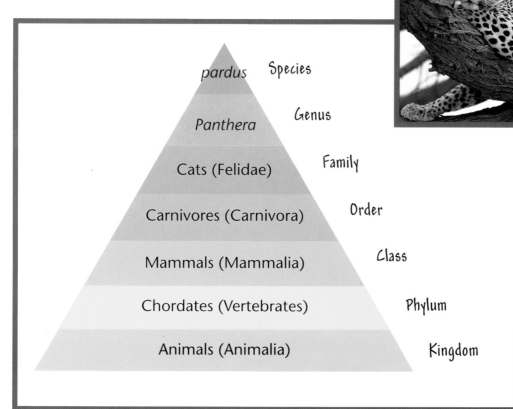

pardus — Species

Panthera — Genus

Cats (Felidae) — Family

Carnivores (Carnivora) — Order

Mammals (Mammalia) — Class

Chordates (Vertebrates) — Phylum

Animals (Animalia) — Kingdom

This diagram shows the full classification for Panthera pardus—a *leopard.*

Furry Milk-drinkers

Within the animal kingdom, mammals are part of a group called the vertebrates. If you feel down the middle of your back, you can feel the bones of your spine, or backbone. These bones are called vertebrae. So vertebrates are animals with backbones. Amphibians, reptiles, birds, and mammals are all vertebrates.

What is a mammal?

Mammals have features in common that separate them from the other groups of vertebrates. Birds have feathers, reptiles are scaly, but mammals are usually hairy or furry. A few, such as humans and whales, have lost much of their hair, but they do have some hair at some point in their lives.

Birds, reptiles, and amphibians lay eggs, but mammals give birth to live babies. However, there are two unusual types of mammals—the platypuses and echidnas—that do lay eggs.

Mammals are **warm-blooded.** This means that their bodies maintain one temperature no matter what the temperature around them may be. Also, all mammal mothers feed their babies on milk made in their **mammary glands.** This is why they are called mammals.

*Mammal milk is full of **nutrients.** Mammal babies, such as this camel, grow quickly on this rich food.*

The first mammals

Around 248 million years ago, even before the first dinosaurs appeared, a great **extinction** took place across the earth. More than 90 percent of all animal **species** died out. Many new types of animals appeared after this extinction. These included dinosaurs and the earliest mammals.

The early mammals were small insect-eaters similar to today's shrews. For millions of years they remained small, while the dinosaurs became the most successful large animals. Then about 65 million years ago, another great extinction wiped out the dinosaurs, but the mammals survived. Many new species soon appeared, because there was no longer competition for food and space from the dinosaurs.

Evolving and adapting

Many scientists believe that over thousands or millions of years, groups of living things may evolve, or change, making them better **adapted** to their **habitat.** This happens because living things that are better adapted to their habitat live longer and produce more offspring. Scientists believe that all mammals have evolved from a single group of **ancestors.**

Early mammals probably looked like this Morganucodon. This is a reconstruction of a mammal that lived during the Jurassic period, about 200 million years ago.

Mammal Orders

There are about 4,600 **species** of mammals. They are grouped into 21 different **orders**.

The orders are shown in the table below.

Order	No. of species	Families
Egg-laying mammals Monotremata	3	platypuses, echidnas
Pouched animals Marsupialia	272	kangaroos, wombats, koalas, opossums, phalangers, wallabies
Placental mammals Rodentia	over 2,000	mice, rats, squirrels, voles, hamsters, beavers, porcupines
Chiroptera	925	bats
Insectivora	375	shrews, moles, hedgehogs
Carnivora	235	cats, dogs, wolves, foxes, badgers, weasels, stoats, mongooses, otters
Primates	233	lemurs, monkeys, apes, humans
Artiodactyla	220	sheep, cattle, pigs, goats, deer, antelopes, pigs, giraffes, camels
Lagomorpha	80	rabbits, hares
Cetacea	79	whales, dolphins, porpoises
Pinnipedia	35	seals, walruses, sea lions
Edentata	29	anteaters, armadillos, sloths
Dermoptera	2	colugos (flying lemurs)
Macroscelidea	19	elephant shrews
Scandentia	19	tree shrews
Perissodactyla	18	horses, zebras, donkeys, rhinos, tapirs
Pholidota	7	pangolins
Hyracoidea	7	hyraxes
Sirenia	4	manatees, dugongs
Proboscidea	3	elephants
Tubulidentata	1	aardvark

Sometimes it is hard to see why a group of species belong to the same order. Weasels and polar bears, for example, do not look much alike, but both are members of the order Carnivora. They are linked by the long teeth in their upper and lower jaws, which work together like a pair of scissors to slice through flesh.

Eggs and pouches

Most mammals give birth to live babies. While the babies grow inside their mothers, they get food from a special **organ** called the placenta. They are called **placental mammals.**

But in two mammal orders, the monotremes and the **marsupials,** things are different. Monotremes are very unusual mammals that lay eggs. There are only three monotreme species: two types of echidnas and the duck-billed platypus. They are found in Australia and New Guinea. Monotremes count as mammals because they are furry and **warm-blooded** and because baby platypuses and echidnas feed on milk from their mother's **mammary glands.**

Marsupials, such as kangaroos and koalas, give birth to live babies, but the newborn babies are extremely tiny and helpless. They spend their first weeks of life in the safety of their mother's pouch.

Echidnas are a little like hedgehogs, because their coat has spines as well as hairs. They eat ants and termites, which they lick up with their long, sticky tongues.

Pouched Mammals

Marsupials are named after the pouch, called a marsupium, in which they carry their babies. They have this pouch because the babies are still very tiny and helpless when they are born and need to be protected from **predators.** Koalas, kangaroos, wombats, bandicoots, phalangers, opossums, and Tasmanian devils are all marsupials. Most marsupials live in Australia, but there are also marsupials in South America and one **species** in North America.

Plugging in to mom

Marsupial babies are the size of bees when they are born. The only part of their bodies that is well developed is one front claw. They use this claw to drag themselves from the birth canal to their mother's pouch. There, each baby fastens itself on to a teat and begins to drink milk. The teat swells in the baby's mouth, so the baby is firmly plugged in to its mother.

Marsupial babies stay in the pouch and feed for four to five weeks. Then they begin to leave the pouch for short periods of time, and they gradually become independent.

Kangaroos produce only 1 baby at a time, but this opossum can produce as many as 25 babies. However, an opossum mother has only 13 teats, so some of the babies do not survive.

A few of the smaller marsupials do not have a pouch, but they still produce undeveloped babies that attach themselves to their mother's teats.

Bigfoot bounders

Kangaroos and wallabies are a **family** of marsupials. All have powerful back legs, large feet, and a long, muscular tail. Most of them graze on grass and are active at night. Because of their huge feet, the family is called the Macropodidae, which means "big feet."

When grazing, a kangaroo moves about on all fours. But when it senses danger, it bounds away on its powerful back legs. A kangaroo's leap can take it 10 feet (3 meters) high and 30 feet (10 meters) ahead. It could clear a couple of cars in one jump.

Phalangers and opossums

Two other groups of marsupials are the phalangers and the opossums. Phalangers are a family of small marsupials found in Australia, where they are called "possums." Opossums are found in South and North America.

Some of these animals have **adapted** well to living alongside humans. This is partly because they are active only at night, and they eat a wide variety of foods. Virginia opossums are famous for "playing possum," or pretending to be dead. They do this to defend themselves against predators.

Chisel-toothed Chewers

Mice, rats, voles, hamsters, squirrels, beavers, and porcupines are all rodents. Rodents are the biggest mammal **order,** with more than 2,000 different **species.**

All rodents have long, strong front teeth called incisors, which they use for gnawing. The front of each incisor has a thin, very hard coating, while the back part of the tooth is a little softer. As a rodent gnaws at its food, the back of the tooth wears away more quickly, leaving the tooth with a razor-sharp edge. Most rodents use their incisors to eat nuts, seeds, leaves, and other plant food.

Fast breeders

Small rodents are a tasty bite for all kinds of **predators.** This is one reason why they live only a short time. Rodents make up for their short lives by producing large numbers of babies very quickly. Hamster mothers have up to 12 babies at once, while a lemming mother can produce more than 100 babies

in 6 months! The babies are tiny, blind, and helpless when they are born, but they grow very quickly. A few rodents, such as beavers and the South American cavies, take longer to produce their babies.

Flying squirrels do not really fly. They have flaps of skin between their front and back legs, which they spread out into "wings" as they leap from tree to tree. They can glide long distances this way.

Rodent lifestyles

To avoid predators, many rodents rest during the day and feed at night. Many burrow into the ground, making holes and tunnels where they can rest in relative safety. Some, like the blind mole rat, spend their whole lives underground. Lemmings live in cold climates, and in the winter they dig tunnels under the snow instead of tunneling into the ground.

Some burrowers live alone, but others live in huge colonies. Hundreds of prairie dogs, for instance, live together in enormous underground towns.

Some rodents are tree-dwellers. Many squirrel species live in trees, but there are also tree rats, tree mice, and even tree porcupines.

Beavers, water rats, water voles, and coypus are all water-living rodents. Beavers and coypus eat only plants, but fish-eating rats are fierce water predators. Beavers are famous for blocking rivers or streams with dams to make lakes, where they build their homes.

Coypus come originally from South America, but people have introduced coypus to Europe and the United States, where they have survived and spread.

Rabbits and hares

Rabbits and hares have large incisor teeth, similar to rodents. But they also have a second pair of smaller incisors. This and other differences mean that rabbits and hares are not rodents. Instead they are close relatives. They are classified in their own order, the lagomorphs.

Long-fingered Fliers

Although birds may rule the air by day, bats are masters of the night sky. Other mammals, such as "flying" squirrels, are good gliders, but bats are the only mammals that have wings and can fly. Unlike birds, which have wings made of feathers, a bat's wings are really just large flaps of skin. The finger bones of the bat's "hands" must be enormously long to support this skin. The name for the bat **order** is Chiroptera, which means "hand wing."

Bats can be divided into two groups: the microbats and the megabats. Microbats are generally smaller and eat insects, while megabats are larger and eat fruit. But the main difference between the groups is that megabats have supersensitive night sight, while microbats use sound to find their way around in the dark.

*A group of grey-headed flying foxes roost together. Almost all bats roost upside down, hanging from a branch, from the wall of a cave, or in a hollow tree trunk. In colder countries, bats **hibernate** in this way.*

Megabats

Megabats are also known as fruit bats. They have furry bodies, large eyes, and a pointed nose. Their faces look like a fox's face, so some fruit bats are also known as flying foxes. They have a good sense of smell as well as good eyesight, and they use their noses to smell out the ripest fruit.

Fruit bats only live in warm, tropical countries, where there is enough fruit for them to eat all year round. During the day, fruit bats roost in large groups, often hanging from the branches of trees.

Microbats

Microbats are also known as insect-eating bats, because nearly all of them feed on insects. They also often live in groups. When female bats are having babies, they gather in colonies of up to twenty million. These colonies usually gather in caves.

Microbats have small eyes because sight is not important to them. They use sound to find their way around in the dark and to catch flying insects. As they fly, the bats send out a string of short, high squeaks. The squeaks are so high that people cannot hear them. These sounds echo off objects around the bats, and their sensitive ears pick up the returning echoes. The bats can use the echoes to create an "echo picture" of the world around them. This is called **echolocation.**

Horseshoe bats make sounds through their nose. The horseshoe shape of their nose concentrates the sounds into a beam. As a bat homes in on an insect, its calls get faster and faster so that it can accurately track the insect.

Insect Specialists

An insectivore is an animal that eats mostly insects. Many mammals are insectivores, but there is also a separate **order** of mammals called Insectivora. Shrews, moles, and hedgehogs are all insectivores. They eat insects, as well as spiders, worms, and other tiny creatures.

This pygmy shrew is tiny, but it has a huge appetite. Small animals lose heat very quickly and must burn a lot of food to keep warm. A small shrew must eat more than three times its own body weight each day to stay alive.

Anteaters and armadillos are also insect-eaters. They belong to a separate order called Edentata, which means "toothless." The sloth is also an edentate, but it only eats plants.

Insectivores

Insectivores are small animals with long, sensitive noses. Most are **nocturnal** and live on the ground or in burrows. They rely more on smell and touch than on their small eyes. Some insectivores are thought to be similar to the early **ancestors** of all **placental mammals.**

Three-quarters of all insectivores are shrews—mouselike creatures with small ears and long noses. They eat insects and other small creatures. Shrews produce a strong smell that keeps many **predators** away, and some **species** have a poisonous bite.

Moles have strong front legs and thick claws designed for digging. They dig deep burrows that have a central chamber and rings of tunnels around it. A mole's favorite food is worms, but it also eats insects and other animals.

Instead of fur, hedgehogs have a coat of sharp spines. When an enemy threatens them, they curl up into a prickly ball. In cooler climates, they **hibernate.**

Toothless mammals

The edentate order is made up of insect-eating anteaters and armadillos, plus sloths, which are plant-eaters. The three groups look very different, but they are closely related. The bones of their lower back are different from those of all other mammals. Anteaters have no teeth, but armadillos and sloths have small, simple, peglike teeth. All have long, strong claws on their front feet.

Anteaters live on the ground or in trees. They eat only ants and termites, licking them up with a long, sticky tongue. Giant anteaters use their strong front claws to break open anthills and termite nests.

Armadillos have armor plating, which protects them from predators. They sleep in burrows by day and roam about at night, using their claws to dig for insects. They can smell insects eight inches (twenty centimeters) below the surface.

Most edentates live in South America, but nine-banded armadillos are found in the southern United States. Nine-banded armadillo mothers usually give birth to quadruplets—four identical armadillo babies.

Hard-toed Runners

Hoofed mammals are built for running. They have long legs and hard, horny hooves that protect their feet as they race along. Although they may not run as fast as some mammals, their hooves allow them to run longer distances.

There are two different **orders** of hoofed mammals. Those of the order Artiodactyla walk on two toes. They include sheep, cattle, goats, pigs, deer, antelopes, camels, giraffes, and hippos. Animals in the other order, Perissodactyla, have an odd number of toes. They walk on either three toes or one toe. Horses, zebras, rhinos, and tapirs are all odd-toed.

Springboks don't rely on just running to escape from predators. They try to warn them off by pronking—doing huge jumps straight up into the air. Scientists think that pronking springboks are telling predators, "I'm really fit and strong; don't waste your energy trying to catch me."

Hoofed mammal lifestyles

Hoofed mammals are all **herbivores.** Many live in open grassland or desert, where they can run fast to escape from big cats and other **predators.** Pigs, deer, and goats live in woodlands or mountain areas, where speed is less important.

Male hoofed mammals often have horns, tusks, or antlers, which they use as weapons and to impress females. **Herds** of hoofed mammals often **migrate** as the seasons change. Their babies can walk and run very soon after they are born. Gnus, for instance, can stand five minutes after they are born, and within a day they can run with the herd.

Tough food

Plant food such as grasses and leaves are tough and do not contain many **nutrients**. Hoofed mammals need a special **digestive system** to break down this food. In odd-toed mammals, the second part of the digestive system—the intestines—is where most **digestion** occurs.

Most even-toed animals are ruminants. This means that they have several stomachs and eat their food twice. First, they eat their food quickly, and it goes into a big pouch called the rumen. Here, millions of **microscopic** creatures break down any tough fibers that the animal itself cannot digest. The food then goes back into the animal's mouth where it chews it again, this time more slowly. This is called chewing the cud. After the ruminant swallows the food a second time, the food goes into another stomach, where normal digestion begins.

Asian giant

The biggest land mammal ever was a rhino-like hoofed animal called *Indricotherium*. It lived 25 to 30 million years ago in the regions of Pakistan, Mongolia, and China. It was twice as tall as an elephant and weighed more than about ten modern rhinos!

Camels walk on two large hoofed toes, which have tough leathery pads underneath. When a camel puts its foot down, the toes spread to keep the animal from sinking into the sand.

Scissor-toothed Hunters

The word *carnivore* means "meat-eater." Many animals are carnivores, but there is also a separate **order** of mammals known as Carnivora. It includes cats, dogs, wolves, foxes, bears, badgers, and weasels. What links all carnivores together is a pair of meat-slicing back teeth called the carnassial teeth. Many carnivores are meat-eaters, but some are **omnivores** and one—the giant panda—is a vegetarian!

Catlike carnivores

Cats, hyenas, mongooses, and civets are all related carnivore families. All of them have retractable claws, which means their claws can be drawn back in. Hyenas have huge back teeth specialized for crunching bones, while mongooses are small, agile hunters that sometimes live together in colonies.

Cats themselves are superb hunters. They have strong jaw muscles for a deadly bite, and their meat-slicing teeth are razor sharp. They have excellent eyesight and good hearing.

Many cats kill their prey with a bite to the back of the neck, using their canines—daggerlike teeth. However, big cats such as this lion kill large prey by clamping their jaws into the front of the animal's throat, suffocating it.

Doglike carnivores

Wolves, foxes, bears, raccoons, and weasels are all doglike carnivores. Unlike cats, they cannot retract their claws.

Wolves, wild dogs, and foxes are all part of the dog **family** itself. The dogs we keep as pets are descended from wolves. Like cats, they are hunters, but they also eat other food. Dogs rely on their sensitive noses to find **prey.** They do not lie in wait but instead chase their prey. Wolves and wild dogs hunt in packs, but foxes hunt alone.

The raccoon family and bear family of carnivores are closely related. Many of them are omnivores. Bears are the biggest of all carnivores. Kodiak and polar bears can weigh up to 2,200 pounds (1,000 kilograms)—as much as a small car!

Weasels, stoats, badgers, and otters are known as mustelids. Most members of this varied family are **predators.** Weasels and stoats have long, flexible bodies for chasing small animals along burrows or hunting them in the water. Badgers are worm specialists, while wolverines are fierce predators that can kill reindeer.

*Giant pandas look like bears but are more closely related to raccoons. They are vegetarians, living almost entirely on bamboo shoots. Pandas are found only in a few places in China. They are among the world's most **endangered** animals.*

Clever-fingered Climbers

Lemurs, monkeys, apes, and humans are all primates. Most live in hot parts of the world, particularly in forests. Many primates are tree-dwellers, but a few **species,** such as baboons and humans, live on the ground. Primates have excellent eyesight and a good sense of touch. Their hands are designed for grasping things, and most have flat nails rather than claws.

Similar bodies, different behavior

Most primates' bodies are not specialized for a particular lifestyle. Their hands and feet, for instance, are still similar to those of their early **ancestors.** Primates have **adapted** to the different places they live by changing their behavior rather than by undergoing body changes. So, although a human hand looks similar to that of a lemur, it is used for quite different activities.

To learn new ways of behaving and to remember them, you need to have a big brain. Primates generally have large, complicated brains.

The majority of primates spend their lives in trees. Smaller monkeys and lemurs, such as this Verreaux's sifaka, run along branches on all fours and leap from one tree to the next. Gibbons, other apes, and larger monkeys often swing from branch to branch instead.

Primate types

The biggest division within the primate **order** is between lemurs and their relatives and the monkeys and apes. Lemurs and related species, such as bush babies, have longer snouts than monkeys and apes do and their noses are wet like a dog's nose. Their eyes are usually large, because most of them are night-feeders, and their ears are large and moveable.

Monkeys have shorter faces and smaller ears than lemurs do, and they have dry noses. Most South American (New World) monkeys can feel and hold onto things with their tails. Monkeys from Africa and Asia (Old World) cannot do this.

Apes include gibbons, orangutans, gorillas, and chimpanzees. They have broad chests and no tails.

Growing and learning

Primate babies have a lot to learn before they can survive by themselves. In addition to learning how to find food and avoid **predators,** they must learn how to fit in with their group. It takes two years for lemurs to become adults and ten years or more for gorillas, chimps, and humans.

Most primates have only one baby at a time. The baby clings to its mother's fur from soon after birth and depends on her for food and care.

Air-breathing Swimmers

Some mammals have **adapted** to life in water. The two biggest **orders** of sea mammals are the seals and walruses (Pinnipedia) and the whales and dolphins (Cetacea).

Flippered carnivores

Some scientists classify seals and walruses as part of the Carnivora order because their **ancestors** are thought to have been similar to bears. But today they look very different from bears. They live in coastal seas, especially in cold polar areas, and their bodies suit their watery lifestyle.

Seals and walruses are streamlined, so they can move quickly through the water. They have small ears or no ears at all. They have a thick layer of blubber, or fat, under their skin that keeps them warm. Their arms and legs have become broad, flat flippers. However, they are not completely adapted to life in the water. They need to breathe air, and their babies are born on land.

Like the **carnivores** on land, seals and walruses eat meat. Seals eat fish, octopuses, crabs, and shrimp. Leopard seals and sea lions eat penguins. Walruses mostly eat shellfish from the seabed.

Up to a million walruses may gather together on a beach in the **breeding** season. Each walrus mother only has one pup. Pups grow quickly on their mother's extra-rich milk and are ready to go to sea after a few weeks.

Whales and dolphins

Whales and dolphins spend their whole lives in water and cannot survive on land. They have no back legs but have developed a tail similar to a fish. In fact, whales and dolphins look a lot more like fish than they look like mammals. But they still need to breathe air, and they feed their babies on milk.

Whales and dolphins can be divided into two groups: the baleen whales and the toothed whales. The largest whales, such as blue whales, fin whales, right whales, and humpback whales, are baleen whales. They are named after the sheets of horny material, called baleen, that they have instead of teeth. To feed, baleen whales either swim through the water with their mouths open or take great gulps of ocean water. The water escapes, but food—shrimp or small fish—gets caught on the baleen and stays in the whale's mouth.

Toothed whales include dolphins, porpoises, killer whales, and sperm whales. They eat all kinds of sea creatures, from shrimp to seals. Killer whales sometimes eat other whales. Sperm whales feed on squid, which they catch from the ocean bottom. They can stay underwater for more than two hours and dive to depths of up to 3,282 feet (1,000 meters).

Sea giant

The blue whale is the largest animal that has ever lived. It can grow to 108 feet (33 meters) in length and weigh 135 tons.

Long-nosed Giants

Elephants are unmistakable. With their long trunks, tusks, and large ears, they are unlike any other animal. Elephants live mainly in grasslands or forests and eat grass, leaves, tree bark, and other plant food. Family groups of females and their babies live together. The groups are led by the oldest female. Male elephants leave their family groups when they are about eight years old and live alone or in all-male groups.

Elephants have long lives. They may live to a ripe old age of 60 or 70. A baby elephant takes time to grow up. It drinks its mother's milk until it is 18 months old, and it is not fully grown until it is about 17 years old.

An elephant can eat up to 662 pounds (300 kilograms) of food a day! Elephant groups travel up to 28 miles (45 kilometers) a day to find food. They often eat day and night, only resting during the middle of the day.

African or Asian?

There are only three **species** of elephants: the African forest elephant, the African grassland elephant, and the Asian elephant. Scientists have only recently discovered that the forest and grassland elephants are separate species. The two types of African elephants are bigger than Asian elephants and have bigger ears.

African elephants are the world's biggest living land animals. They weigh up to 7.5 tons—as much as a small truck!

Elephant trunks

An elephant's trunk has many uses. It can be used to smell the breeze or sniff for underground water. The end of the trunk is very sensitive and can pick up small objects. (The trunk of an African elephant ends in two "fingers," but an Asian elephant has only one.) The trunk is also very strong and can carry heavy things such as tree trunks. Elephants can suck up water or dust in their trunks and spray it out to give themselves a shower or dust bath. They also make noises through their trunks to communicate with each other.

Ivory teeth

An elephant's tusks are overgrown front teeth, which can grow many feet long. Elephants use them to dig for water, scrape bark from tree trunks, or break down small trees. Males sometimes also use their tusks when they fight over a female. Elephant tusks are made of ivory. Killing elephants for their ivory is no longer allowed, but some people, called poachers, illegally kill thousands of elephants each year.

Asian elephants have been used as working animals for hundreds of years. They are still used today in parts of India, Myanmar, and Thailand.

An elephant has only four huge molars for chewing food—two above and two below. Although these teeth are very hard, they do slowly wear down. Once they are worn down, a new set of molars replaces them. Altogether an elephant has six sets of molars. When the sixth pair is worn down, the elephant can no longer eat properly and eventually starves.

Is It a Mammal or Not?

We have seen that most mammals are hairy or furry, are **warm-blooded,** and feed their babies on milk. But some mammals have become so completely specialized for the life they lead that they don't seem to be mammals at all!

Fishy mammals

Dolphins and other toothed whales look similar to some fish, especially sharks. Like sharks, dolphins have streamlined bodies, fins, and a tail. Dolphins have up to 300 teeth, and sharks also have many teeth. Dolphins give birth to live babies, and some types of sharks do too. These similarities are mostly due to the fact that both sharks and dolphins are ocean **predators.** They need to be able to move quickly through the water and catch their **prey.**

Certain differences between sharks and dolphins, however, make it clear that they belong to separate **classes.** Like all fish, sharks have gills and get the oxygen they need from water, while dolphins have lungs and must breathe air. Sharks cannot keep their bodies warm in cold water, but a dolphin's body temperature stays much the same no matter how warm or cold the water is. Also, shark babies have to take care of themselves as soon as they are born, but dolphin mothers feed their babies on milk from their **mammary glands.**

Sharks such as this mako shark look similar to dolphins and porpoises. However, the shark's gill slits show that it gets its oxygen from water rather than from air.

The pangolin's scales make it look more like a reptile than a mammal. It curls up into a ball if attacked.

Flying mammals

In a similar way, bats have some similarities to birds because both animals have been **adapted** for flying. Both birds and bats have wings. And both are limited in how big they can grow, because they cannot become too heavy to fly. But birds have feathers and beaks, while bats have furry bodies and a mouth with teeth. Also, birds lay eggs, while bats give birth to live babies and feed them on milk.

Scaly mammals

Pangolins (**order** Pholidota) live in Africa and southern Asia. They have long noses and strong, clawed feet, and the tops of their bodies are covered in overlapping scales. They feed at night on ants and termites, which they dig out with their strong legs and lick up with their long tongue.

Because of their scales, you might think that pangolins are reptiles. But in fact they are mammals. They give birth to live babies, are warm-blooded, and feed their babies on milk. Their scales are actually made from hairs.

Glossary

adaptation special feature that helps an organism to survive in its habitat

ancestor relative from long in the past

breed to produce babies

carnivore animal that eats meat

cell smallest unit of life. Most animals are made up of millions of cells.

class level of classification grouping between phylum and order. Mammals make up a class.

digestion process by which an animal breaks down food so that it can be absorbed into the body

digestive system part of an animal's body that breaks down food so that it can be used by the body

echolocation system that animals such as bats use to "see" by making sounds and listening to their echoes

endangered in danger of becoming extinct

extinction dying out of an entire species or group of species

family level of classification grouping between order and genus

fossil remains of ancient living creatures (usually formed from bones or shells) found in rocks

gene substance by which all living things pass on characteristics from one generation to the next

genus (plural is **genera**) level of classification grouping between family and species

habitat place where a group of animals live most of the time

herbivore animal that eats only plants

hibernate to sleep through the winter

mammary gland milk-producing gland used to feed babies, found on the belly or the chest of a female mammal

marsupial type of mammal whose babies are born tiny and must stay in a pouch on the mother's stomach

microscopic too small to be seen with the naked eye

migrate to move from one place to another for part of the year

nocturnal active at night

nutrient chemical from food that nourishes our bodies

omnivore animal that eats both plants and animals

order level of classification grouping between class and family

organ part of the body that does a particular job

phylum (plural **phyla**) level of classification grouping between kingdom and class

placental mammal mammal that gives birth to well-developed babies

predator animal that hunts other animals for food

prey animals that are hunted by other animals for food

species lowest level of classification grouping. Only members of the same species can reproduce together.

warm-blooded able to keep the body temperature about the same, even when the surroundings are colder or hotter

More Books to Read

Claybourne, Anna. *Mammals.* Brookfield, Conn.: Millbrook Press, Incorporated, 2000.

Green, Jen. *Mammals.* Austin, Tex.: Raintree Publishers, 2002.

Parker, Steve. *Adaptation.* Chicago: Heinemann Library, 2000.

Wallace, Holly. *Classification.* Chicago: Heinemann Library, 2000.

Index